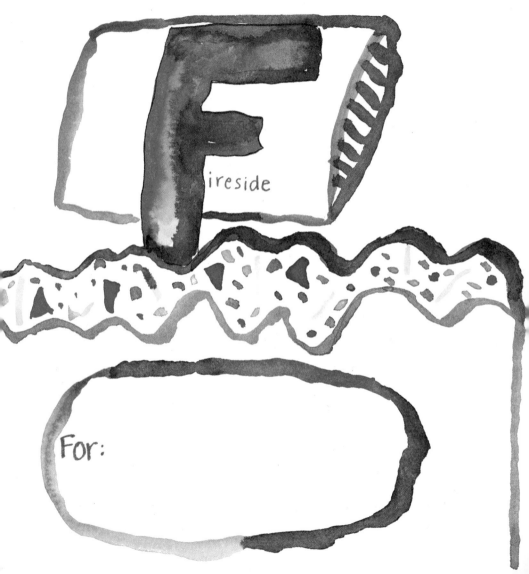

Fireside

For:

THE BODACIOUS BOOK of Succulence

SUCCULENT WILD WOMAN
Also an AUDIO TAPE

THE MAGIC COTTAGE ADDRESS BOOK

SARK's JOURNAL :PLAY: BOOK

A CREATIVE Companion
Also an AUDIO TAPE

inspiration Sandwich

LIVING JUICY

OTHER BOOKS BY SARK

Yes, and MORE BOOKS TO COME

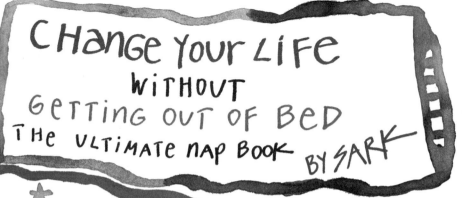

# CHANGE YOUR LIFE WITHOUT GETTING OUT OF BED
## THE ULTIMATE NAP BOOK
### BY SARK

A
Fireside
BOOK
PUBLISHED
BY
SIMON & SCHUSTER

Jupiter is in the house

**F**
Fireside
Rockefeller Center
1230 Avenue of the Americas
new york, new york 10020

This book is dedicated to MY MOM "Marvelous Marjorie" Who made the ultimate parental sleep sacrifices and would have read a lot more books if she could have stayed up all night! Mom, thanks for being a great role model and horizontal parent I love you

Permission for the Rumi Quote on page 82 Originally published by Threshold Books 139 Main St. Brattleboro VT 05301

A lilting thank you to: The radiant Trish The spirited Marcela The incandescent Cherlynne The sensitive Jim The beatific Mark

Fireside and Colophon are registered trademarks of Simon & Schuster Inc.
Simon & Schuster lets SARK draw their symbol just for this book! They are a fair and generous publisher

Manufactured in the United States of America By kind and loving souls
10  9  8  7  6  5  4  3  2  1
These are the numbers for how many times the book is printed

A special color filled thank you to the rare & marvelous Andrea Scher, who provided so much luminous assistance and support during the creation of this book. Senior designer, Camp SARK
EACH BOOK is created with the help of many hearts and hands. I deeply thank my two business partners, Adrienne Steele and Brigette Scheel, whose vision and creative input added so much great stuff to this book and to this author! Thank you also to Jason and Tanya at Camp SARK, whose wit and humor lift us all up. Also Bless each volunteer! Thank you to the creative culture and my two agents, Debra Goldstein and Mary Ann Naples, whose insights are deeply felt & appreciated

Library of Congress Catalog Card Number: 98-53161
Library of Congress Cataloging-in-Publication Data is available The Library of Congress needs a nap room, I'm sure
ISBN 0-684-85930-0

# A BIG STACK of PILLOWS

naps fluff us up and make us more kind. Use this book as your private nap support system. It works especially well if you allow it to seep in while you're sleeping!

My life is one long nap, punctuated by brief moments of activity.

I hope to see you in Napland!

6

reasons
TO
NAP

THE FLYING Pillow

9

THIS BOOK is BEING WRITTEN BY A PERSON WHO ~~SOMETIMES~~ USUALLY resists, AVOIDS AND FEARS CHANGE. I DON'T THINK THAT THIS MATTERS.

AS MY FRIEND REBECCA LATIMER, Author of You're Not Old Until you're ninety, SAYS,

"I'M A rotten Meditator! I JUST DO it ANYWAY, AND it still WORKS."

SO, I DON'T GRACEFULLY ACCEPT CHANGE Most of the time, AND yet it still works.

CHANGE DOESN'T CARE if we ACCEPT or resist it. I HAPPEN to Believe THAT tAKING lots of NAPS Along the WAY, FACILITATES THE CHANGES.

CHANGING Your LIFE CAN HAPPEN WHEN you're Not trying so HArD, or WHEN you're Asleep!

I THINK THAT CHANGE OFTEN slips in WHEN
10  we're relaxed inside of ourselves.

THe process of truly Becoming yourself TAKes A lot of energy, and this energy can Be replenished During naps.

This Book can Be tucked under your pillow and it will induce naps.

Inside Are:

NAp Permission slips, Great nap places, nap clothes, nap exercises, **ways to make more money** while napping, napping without guilt, special naps for parents, suggestions and games for making changes in your life and more...

My First and Best Job was As the wake up Fairy in Kindergarten.

I HAD A MAGIC wand and touched each sleeping child on the HEAD with it.

They Awoke From their nap to have little cups of Juice and A cookie.

sometimes you could get extra

As adults, we still need these nap-times. We need tender places in which to repair our souls and put special glue on the broken places

cloud cover

12

We replenish and repair during naps.
   Even if you don't actually sleep, setting up for a nap provides an atmosphere of safety and kindness for the interior.

Napping softens all the edges and S M O O T H E S the shredded places.

Naps are the ADULT version of a CHILD'S Fort. A love of privacy and place for MAKE-Believe.

I Believe I can Do it Now

rest ADDS strength to our souls.

SAIL
YOUR
DREAM
SHIP TO
the
laND
OF
NAP

14

# Permission

## For:

## TO NAP ALL DAY

Pleasures
and
Benefits
of NAPPING

# Pleasures and Benefits
## of Napping
### and relaxing

Joy-Full, Flexible, Buoyant Humans!

17

> "There is a dream, dreaming you."
> Aboriginal Saying

People who nap are often more creatively awake. Napping—especially while dreaming lucidly—can set the stage for outbursts of creativity.

I often nap before writing or painting, and find new shapes, colors or words dancing around after I awaken.

I know that the contact with the subconscious creates a "creative chamber" for new things to be born into.

Writing, scribbling, drawing or singing when you awaken from this sort of nap can help give shape to splendid new forms of creativity

LOVErs WHo nAp TOGether CreATE an ADDitionAL Sleep Time to CoMMuNiCATE in. We Can ConNecT WiTH EACH oTHer in DreAMS.

It can Also Be Glorious To nAp wiTH FrieNds, in THe sAMe House, rooM, BeD or HouseBOAT. nAppiNG wiTH FrieNds can Be enDeAriNG and iNtiMATe. Seeing A Friend in A "nAppisH" MooD Deepens The FriendsHip.

THe MoVie <u>THe</u> <u>WizArd</u> of <u>OZ</u> proMotes nAps WHen DoroTHy lies DoWN in THe FieLD of poppies, and THen rewArds Her fir sleepiNG

BY PutTinG Her Closer To THe emerALD CiTY

TeA · nAps Are another MArvelous thing

sleep · Time

HAve teA and too Many cookies
and THen DriFT off on FAT pillows WHile
Someone tells sTories.

NAps COULD UJe More Group Activity!
We COULD ForM neigHBorHooD nAp Groups
and HAve nAp stickers

or, BUMper stickers

N A P
Friendly
HoMe

I'M a nApper
PleAse Drive Gently
20

I AM OBViously an ADVOCATE of
NAPS
If you Like naps, speak up About it!
SHARe naps, nap stories anD nap
encourAGeMent With others.

21

Permission

For:

To NAP ABUNDANTLY

22

THE
MORE NAPS
YOU TAKE,
THE MORE
MONEY YOU'LL MAKE

THE MORE NAPS YOU TAKE

in spirit we TRUST

THE MORE MONEY YOU'LL MAKE!

During my many years as a starving artist and rejected creative person, I retreated often to naps to restore my sanity.

I often sailed away to naps to repair from my perfectionism, procrastination or the voices of the inner critics shouting at me:

"You're Broke!"

"you'll never make it!"

"others have money, not you!"

These naps were a resting place to heal the broken places and go forward with life again.

I now know that the more relaxed and trusting we can be with money, the more it can flow for us.

I THINK THAT the energy of MONEY runs AWAY FROM worry, and THAT our enduring JOB is TO nurture and re-parent ourselves — especially in the rEALM of MONEY.

"WORRY is NOT prepARATION."
CHERI HUBER

BUILD A TreeHouse

PAint your HAir

SInG To an angel

Create A Mystery

Support A Miracle

Be Gentle ABout Money

SWIM BY MOONLIGHT

invent A New WorLD

EAT inspiring FOOD

lie Down and let your IMAGINATION SPEAK

I can hear you now, wondering how and
if this applies to you.

Try an experiment. Do two things.

1. Buy a money book (your choice, or 2 suggestions)
   Creating Money by Sanaya Roman & Duane Packer
   Nine Steps to Financial Freedom by Suze Orman

   Read a sentence or paragraph daily for 30 days.

2. Increase your nap quantity— double or triple
   if you can— they can be miniature or micronaps.
   Do a 30-day experiment.

Write in a notebook or journal what your
findings are.

   * I found that both my relaxation and
     money flow increased.

Our very own lives are the best things to
experiment on!

You deserve to relax and have money

27

Try This: Use my Affirmation if you Like it:

> The More Naps I Take, the More Money I Make.

Use it for 30 Days and Just see What Serendipitous Things Have Happened with money and/or naps. I Believe That we must be The True source of our Funds, and That The Money energy willingly sent out returns to us many times over. It is the clutching or Fear that can Block The Flow. I still get scared, Forget to Breathe and meditate, or take trusting naps.

invent A Flying carpet and use it to Float over any perceived obstacles

I send us All more money and more naps!

28

Permission

For:

TO HAVE naps and Money

29

Great
Nap
places

nap
craft

SAIL
THROUGH
A relaxing SEA
TO A STATE
of DREAMS

31

# Tree·naps

Naps in trees are good, because after you hug a tree, you can nap in it! The leaves can be the walls of your tree bedroom, wide branches are your bed.

Trees rustle like bedclothes, and at the right angle, you can feel like you're flying or sailing during your tree·nap.

I think it must be comforting for a tree to be napped in. If I were a tree, I would welcome people napping in my branches.

Children can still hear trees talking (we can too, if we will only listen).

I sometimes imagine that I hear the trees murmuring invitations to me as I walk through the woods.     Try a tree·nap!

Plane·naps often originate from boredom or despair, or an intense desire to escape a sound, smell, or sense of claustrophobia.

This can actually be the preface to an unexpectedly marvelous nap. There is nothing quite like falling asleep in one country and waking up in another!

plane·naps

For me, the ideal plane·nap occurs when I've been able to secure 3 seats across, 3-6 pillows and as many blankets.

We all know the challenges of the window seat wedge — pillow or clothing up against the window.

One of the most advanced nap techniques occurs in the middle seat, with a person on each side of you, one of them a baby.

I've also had successful naps on top of my backpack, on top of the tray table.

Drooling is allowed during plane·naps!

I think that MOST OF US HAVE CHILDHOOD CAR-NAP memories. I remember BLANKETS SMELLING of CAR LEATHER and The murmur of my PARENTS' VOICES BLENDING WITH The HUMMING sounds of ROAD and CAR. To This DAY, Motion puts Me to sleep. I love CURLING up For A CAR-NAP with any HANDY SWEATER or BLANKET, someone I TRUST Driving and HOURS AHEAD TO NAP.

One time, my Brother and I HAD settled in For A DAYTIME CAR-NAP in YOSEMITE, By The side of The ROAD. We put clean SOCKS over our eyes to BLOCK out THE LIGHT. I woke up DROOLING, and looked over to see my Brother DROOLING, too! I woke Him up with my LAUGHTER, WHICH ended When we Discovered The CAR BATTERY HAD Died!

A JARRING end TO A GOOD CAR-NAP.

34

CAR-NAPS

## BEACH. NAPS

Sand Must Be Accepted To enjoy a Beach·nap. Blowing Sand can Be Hidden From, except it will Always Show up in Between your teeth.

While Lying on your stomach, Warm sun on your Back, you can Glide into A Deep and rapturous nap. Beach·napping can Be elusive, But utterly Bliss·full.

Grass·naps Are Awesome in long, springy, Fresh Green Grass. Tiny Daisies Are Good company too. Let The Fragrance of Grass surround you As you nap.

You can Grass·nap without any Accessories, including A Blanket. let The Grass Cradle you.

Grass·naps Are Fun with children and animals.

You can play tickle Grass Games too.

Grass is Like The Hair of The earth!

## GrASS·nAPS

# @ Permission

For:

TO NAP WHErever you want To! @

nap
without
guilt

37

let's MAGNIFY OUR CLOCKS of Forgiveness

Yes

no worries

Go Without Me

ACTUALLY, I DON'T FEEL LIKE IT

it's O.K

NAP

sleep

Quit

it's O.K.

GO BACK TO sleep

CALL later

NAP

CLOCK of Forgiveness

THE HAVE TO CLOCK

Hurry
Mistake
SHOULD
WORRY
WORRY
NO HAVE to
WRONG

OUR Lives Are Full of CHoices
YOU can CHoose to NAp

lie Down in the MiDST of Avoidance

NAPPiNG WithOUT GUiLT TAKes COuRAGe, pRActice and DeterMiNAtion.

People JuDGe THeMselves for NAPPiNG (or wanting to NAP) and others for NAPPiNG.

My Friend BriGette jusT ADMitted THAt SHe JuDGeD Her College roomMAtes for TAKiNG DAiLy nAPs, and THOUGHT it MeaNT THAT THey were Depressed. SHe and I Grew up in THe MiDWesT, wHere nAPs Are liNKeD with LAZiness and lACK of MotivAtion too.

WHAt is THAt AWFUL SAYiNG: "idle HanDs Are THe Devils WorKSHop"? THese KiNDs of words and eNerGy HeLp To promote our CULTure of over·DoiNG insteAD of BeiNG.

Society HAS not Known HOw or wHy to support nAps ÷ I'M GLAD THis is CHanGiNG!

# Guilt·Free Nap exercises

Here Are some suggestions for napping without (or with less) guilt.

- realize THAT you Now HAVe permission To lie Down and nap ÷ for no reason!
- encourage others to nap, and form nap· support friendships.
- refuse to Accept any judgments About napping from yourself or others.
- Speak openly and often About The pleasures and Benefits of napping.

- Be Seen By and with other nappers.
You can Appoint A nap angel in your own Life!

WE HAVE THE RIGHT TO NAP WHEN WE CHOOSE, FOR AS LONG AS WE CHOOSE, with no explanations or JUSTIFICATIONS! I AM AMAZED BY HOW MANY PEOPLE DON'T NAP BECAUSE OF GUILT, or secretly NAP BECAUSE of GUILT. I THINK THAT NAPS GOT MIXED UP WITH SIN SOMEWHERE ALONG THE WAY.

MY FRIEND CRAIG CAN NAP ANYWHERE, ANYTIME. He once NAPPED IN FULL PUBLIC VIEW ON A MEATSCALE AT A TRAIN STATION IN MOROCCO.

He ALSO NAPPED IN MY BOOTH AT A BOOK FESTIVAL ON MY PURPLE CHAISE LOUNGE,

nAPS Forever

As Hundreds of people walked past. So many
people came up and said in awed voices,
"is He really napping? Just like that? So
Freely out in public?"

Purple chaise lounges
can sometimes have
that effect

We must reclaim our Napping selves!
We must work against nap guilt Wherever we
Find it, Become part of the Nap revolution
and turn the whole world into a free nap zone.
(Oh my, I'm sounding a bit nap fanatic)!

Hiding the fact that we nap can
Happen when people have been repressed
For years by

# NAPGUILT

permission

For:

TO NAP GUILT·FREE

43

Fantasy
NAPS
Naps for
Parents

44

# Fantasy Naps

WHere HAVe yOU HAD GReAT nAps, or
AlWAys wanted to nAp? ADD your own
words,
Here!

WHere HAVe you Always wanted to NAP?

ID Like To nAP in A BANK line, A Dentist's Office and A plush corner of A busy Department store.

For some reason, I've never nApped in A HAMMOCK! I Think This cAMe From an early HAMMOCK TrAuMA, WHen A HAMMOCK collApsed and crAsHed To The Ground with me in it.

I'M Going to see if I can HAVe A successFul HAMMOCK nAp sometime This year.

I'll let you know.

One of My Best FanTAsy nAps HAppened with A Friend I went HiKing with.

We Arrived in His
Truck at the
Trailhead and
Climbed into the
Back to get our
Backpacks and
Boots.
I don't remember
who
laid
down
first in
the back
of that truck,
But when we woke
up 4 Hours later, the
sun had set!

We had Hiked to Nap land.

NAP land

47

# nAps For pArents

One of the reasons I Didn't BecOMe A pArent WAS Because of the lAck of sleep. I Give HuGe AMounts of credit to any pArent reADinG This. The pArenting sleep sAcrifice is HuGe and pArents Deserve Deferred nAp·TiMe For Their Contribution. 1st priz 1st prize

My iDEA is MMM MicrO·nAps. Tiny, tiny, itty Bitty nAplets in The MidST of A Busy DAy. My DeAr Friend Ken, FATHer of Zoe, illustrAtes This:

"pILe All the pillows on Top of DADDY, and see How long it TAkes you!"
→ CHAnce For A micrO·nAp

Micro·nAPPinG DADDY

There is another chance for naps for parents and this is called Family Nap. This is where parent(s) and child(ren) pile into bed at any time of day or night, to sing songs, tell stories, play games and hopefully... take a micro-nap!

I remember my mom taking daily naps. She revealed years later that she had been mostly nocturnal and was up all night reading books! I think that parents could have "date nights" where they get a babysitter and go to a motel or friend's house

FAMILY NAP

JUST TO NAP

# Permission

For:

## TO MICRO·NAP A lot

nap
equipment
nap
clothes

51

MAGIC BLANKET

lucky PAJAMAS

Perfect Pillow

COZY SOCKS

Our Lives Are Filled With Gorgeous Moments
The smell of clothes Dried in the sun is one of THose.
Relax, and let MOMENTS Like THese seep into your SOUL.

# NAP eQuipmeNt

ear plugs

One of The Best eye pillows MADE is By BUCKY — The people who MAKE The Flaxseed neck pillows. This eye pillow is DARK and puffy and comes with earplugs in Their own cute little pouch.

EARPLUGS Are A Blessing on Airplanes or anywhere There is noise - especially in The DAYTime. My FAvorites Are Silicone and can Be MAPE SMAller For Different-sized ears.

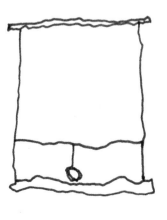

really excellent BLACKout SHADes Are rare and A Definite Help For A Deep nap. I still recall A Hotel suite I rented once with Such Good SHADes, I Couldn't see My Hand (or anything else) in The perfect DARKness. My "nap" lasted 11 Hours!

Pillows Are immensely important to A Good nAp. Many of us MAKe Do with OLD pillows, inHerited pillows or pillows left over From OLD relAtionsHips. Perfect nAp pillows Are not too Costly and will contriBute GreAtly to your nAp stAte.

I use A COMBINATION: Down, Cotton, and Child's Flannel

Sleep socks Can Be A cozy nAp ADDition! I Like wHite, overly roomy ones.

For Hotel rooms without BLACKout sHADes and only polyester curtains and vinyl sHADes, I CArry clothespins to pin togeTher The MAteriAL so THAt less LiGHt Gets in.

They MAKe clothespins in BriGHt colors now!

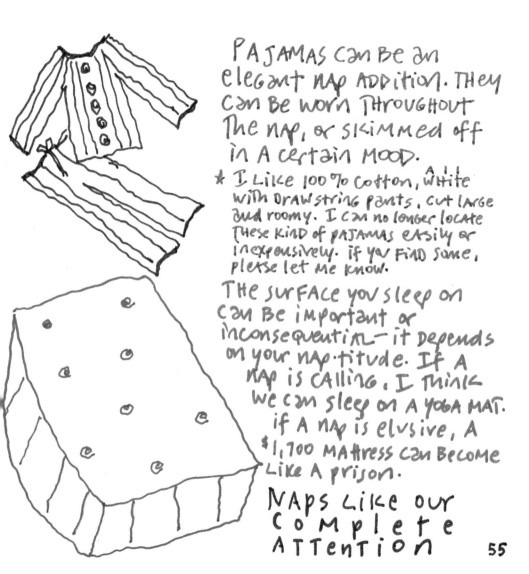

PAJAMAS CAN BE AN
ELEGANT NAP ADDITION. THEY
CAN BE WORN THROUGHOUT
THE NAP, OR SKIMMED OFF
IN A CERTAIN MOOD.

* I LIKE 100% COTTON, ALL WHITE
WITH DRAWSTRING PANTS, CUT LARGE
AND ROOMY. I CAN NO LONGER LOCATE
THESE KIND OF PAJAMAS EASILY OR
INEXPENSIVELY. IF YOU FIND SOME,
PLEASE LET ME KNOW.

THE SURFACE YOU SLEEP ON
CAN BE IMPORTANT OR
INCONSEQUENTIAL — IT DEPENDS
ON YOUR NAP·TITUDE. IF A
NAP IS CALLING, I THINK
WE CAN SLEEP ON A YOGA MAT.
IF A NAP IS ELUSIVE, A
$1,700 MATTRESS CAN BECOME
LIKE A PRISON.

NAPS LIKE OUR
C O M P L E T E
ATTENTION        55

REMEMBER PAJAMAS WITH FEET? THE FEET
HAD little WHITE BUMPS THAT GRIPPED ONTO EVERYTHING.

# B l a n k e t s

Are the outerwear of
naps. A Good Blanket will
Surround you During your
nap and pull you Deeper
into a Dream state.

* I Like pure white cotton
comforters or brightly
Colored comforter covers

A BIG STACK OF HEAVY
Blankets can Be very
comforting too!

# Permission

For:

To invest
in nap clothes & equipment

NAP HAPPY
PEOPLE
nAP COmpanions

# THE CALM BED

We lie in our safe warm
bed pockets and feel our very
cells smiling. stretching our souls
in the dream worlds, our fears uncoil

# nAp companions

one of My Best nAp companions is My
CAT Jupiter. He sleeps circular, or upside Down,
or tucked into The sHeets with His
little BLACK HeAD on The pillow.
USUAlly The siGHT of HiM
nAppinG lures Me into A
nAp, even if I've Just
Gotten up!

I Get envious of His animAl nap cApacity
and remind Him often How lucky He is
To NAp All The time.

I remember my DoG nAp companions too...
Under The covers or Like SofT STones AT THe
end of The Bed.

animAls nAp GuilT-Free, with complete
Trust and ABandon.

We can Join THem More often in nApland!

YOU can spot A
"NAP HAppy" person By
THeir tendency To
BeCOMe Horizontal in
ALMOST every situation.

THey Are often Found seeking
pillows or nap nests

My Brother andrew naps Beatifically on His
BACK, Hands Folded and A slight smile on
His FACe.

He says, "one of My Most FAVorite Moments
in life is Just Before sleep, in that MAGiC
instant Just prior to Drifting off, I usually
Manage to say out loud or think,

'Here... I ... GO...'"

My GrandFATHer WAS SucH A Deep napper
THAT All The CHiLDren were WArned not to
AbruptLY AWAKen Him BecAuse He MiGHT
unKnowingly reAct with FLAiLinG ArMs
or legs.
My DAD WAS A secreT nApper, WHo JerKeD
FAlsely AWAKe WHen you cAme in THe room
And Muttered,
"I WASnT ASleep!"   THere Are As Many nAp
                    Styles As THere Are people

let ribbons of NAP energy move THrough you

NAp HAppy people Are
Found All over THe
WORLD. JUST THinK:
riGHT THis Moment, so
Many people Are nAppinG.
   All over our WORLD

NAPPING is an ART THAT TAKES lots of practice
There Are So Many kinds of naps:

The Miniature nap:     Usually 5-20 Minutes
The Micro·nap:         1-5 Minutes
The DECADENT NAP:     Naked, Blowing curtains, After sex
The Deep & endless nap: 3-5 Hours, Bliss
The CRABBY nap:        Hot pillows, twisting Blankets, noise
The elusive nap:       Hopeless, whining, sighs of Frustration
The Helpless nap:      Unexpectedly pinned to the Bed
                       By your total need To NAP
The DREAMING NAP:      Napping to Have, or stay in, A DREAM
The HEALING nap:       To refresh, replenish, restore
The perfect nap:       Your FAvorite kind
The Multiple nap:      A series of naps in A 24·Hr. period
The SUDDEN nap:        Having to Nap AS <u>soon</u> AS <u>possible</u>
The CHURCH nap:        irresistible

63

permission

For:

TO BE VERY NAP HAPPY

nap
excuses

65

CHOOSE A location

PICK YOUR EQUIPMENT

ON YOUR MARK, GET SET, NAP !!!

SOME people Are Determined to MAKE excuses NOT To NAP, or THey HAVe Not HAD nap success. Here Are some Common excuses:

1. "I've Just never Been ABle To nAp"

2. "I Always WAKe up: 1. GroGGy
   2. CrABBy 3. useless 4. FeeBle"

3. "NAppinG seems inDULGent"

4. "IM Too Busy To NAp"

5. "nAppinG is for others, not Me"

THere Are people WHo Are physicAlly MADe To sleep in longer seGMents. if you HAve TruLy experiMenteD witH naps and it Doesn't Work, you Can Be A NAp ADMirer.

# Nap Suggestions
## lie Down and read These

1. no one can or wants to make you nap. if you're inclined to nap, experiment on yourself with location, equipment and time. There is no wrong way to nap.

2. if you wake up from naps groggy, crabby, feeble or useless, see page ___70___.

3. if you think napping seems indulgent, trace back where this thought came from.
   A. school
   B. church
   C. parents
   D. a nightmare
   e. Deranged Thinking

4. if you think you're too BUSY TO NAP...
   anti-nap DeMons HAve invaded your
   BrAin and intervention is needed.
   See PAGE ___73___.

5. if you still Think you're too BuSy to
   nap. consider GiVing up and GiVe
   This Book AwAy to SoMeone WHo Wants
   To nap. You can Be A nap aDVocATe
   For others.

6. All creatures nAtuRAlly nap.
   even you. if you choose to!

We Are All nAp sTArs anp ancels

SPECIAL PAGE FOR PEOPLE WHO WAKE UP GROGGY
From NAPS

Synchronized napping is part of THE ART.

experiment with How long you NAP, and try WAKING up AT 30-60-90-minute intervals. if you need to nap miniature or micro, Do it AT 5-10-15 minutes. YOUR BODY RHYTHMS Are very sensitive to sleep/AWAKE stages, and Grogginess is usually A sign of WAKING UP AT the wrong time For your BODY.

You can ADD the Art of napping to your sleep skills and still Be Able to sleep At night. It just takes practice and experimentation.

After-nap Clarity Awaits you!

Permission

For:

To be an inspired mapper

Dangers
of
NAP
Deprivation

72

73

YOU can Tell wHen you're nAp DepriveD, BecAUse
THe CRABBY Appletons come out!

THe CRABBY Appletons

and THeir kids!

CRABBY kips

remember: we regress in age wHen we HAVe nt HAD enough sleep!

NAp DeprivAtion is rAMpant in AMericA.
OTHer countries HAVe siestAs. In
InDiA, people wrAp up in BrigHt cloths
anD lie Down in puBLic.

A BrigHt cloth can Be A BeD

In AMericA, people Keep on

D O i n G anD G O i n G

anD BeCoMe very crABBy witHout nAps.

CRABBYAppletons

We've all been exposed to the nap-deprived workers of America.

It results in snippy, frosty, spacey treatment.

These people often simply need a nap!

Airports, corporations, amusement parks and libraries all need nap rooms or nap areas. Schools would benefit greatly from nap rooms.

More naps would result in greater safety, more money and happier people.

Life revolves with our NAP energy

NAP ROOMS
WITH BEDS LIKE
COOL POCKETS...
PLACES TO SLIP INTO
and SLIDE INTO
A DREAM...

# NAP FACTS

- Before the LIGHTBULB WAS invented in 1879, people slept an average of 10 hours a night. now it's about 7 (if that).

- we spend about 18 Billion Dollars A year on accidents and other results of sleep deprivation.

- Trends Research Institute says that napping will soon be one of the top·10 trends.

- There is a national sleep foundation in Washington, and something called The cockpit rest study at NASA.

- More corporations are creating nap rooms, tents and corners, and admitting that napping is productive!

We still need A national nap·support Foundation and more nap Awareness.

NAP
Quotes
nAP
stories

79

nap on!

YOU HAVE permission

80

"START
SLOW
and
TAPer off."
WALT STACK

"TO
rest
is
A
SACreD ACT."
Robyn Posin

"LiFe is A series
of
relapses and recoveries."
George ADe

81

"WHEN I WORK, I WORK HARD.
WHEN I SIT, I SIT LOOSE. AND WHEN
I WORRY, I FALL ASLEEP."
A 100-YEAR-OLD WOMAN
WHEN ASKED ABOUT HER
LONGEVITY

"PART OF THE SELF LEAVES
THE BODY WHEN WE SLEEP AND
CHANGES SHAPE. YOU MIGHT SAY,
'LAST NIGHT I WAS A CYPRESS TREE,
A SMALL BED OF TULIPS, A
FIELD OF GRAPEVINES.'"
RUMI

82

# WHere the NAP TAKes YOU

My nap History is lonG & volumi2ous.
I AM A voluptuous nApper an2 an
extrAvAGant lounGer.

One of MY MOST MAGnificent
nAps Took place on THe Rhine
River in GerMany, AFTer Drinking
A Bottle of wine By Myself.

I sank My HEAD DOwn on the wooden
TAble in an enraptured HAZe, To Be
STartled AwAKe By A sharp Tapping noise.

It wAs The cane of The riverBOAT
Conducter who loudly pronounced,
"no nApping Allowed Here!"
I AM Sure THAT His naps HAVe Been interrupted
ever since.

## A CrveL WISH

Another Great nap took place on my first day in San Francisco, at the Great Meadow near Fort Mason. I found a kind·looking crooked tree, and curled up near it with my sleeping bag.

(The youth Hostel closes daily from 10-5. perhaps they could consider remaining open for nappers during the day.)

I awakened to something very large near my face and a snorting sound.

It was a Horse's Hoof and a Horse's snort and on top of the Horse was a police officer who shouted, "No Napping in the park!"

I quietly said,

"I simply must nap. Please Be kind."

After a long silence, he rode off.

His naps are long and pleasant, I am sure.

84

 Permission

For:

TO GO WHERE THE NAP TAKES YOU

85

napping
is
productive

Declare your Home A Free nap zone!

let nap energy — we welcome nappers — Flow in and out of your Home

All paths lead to ...nap

THE solace of A good nap
MAKES A BASE For new THings
To Grow inside of us.
THis GROWTH leads to change.
THis change leads to:

88 Fill in Your Most needed change

We Are eACH HOLY and ordinary creatures, stumbling Along, leading rare and pathetic lives.

We eACH ASSUMe We Are Alone.

We Are NOT.

I Believe that telepathy occurs During naps. We can Also receive spiritual gifts During naps.

WHAT CHange(s) Are you Most AFrAid/reluctant To MAke?

If you can speak or write About your CHanges, you will Find Companions searching for The same Things, and profoundly realize THAT   Y O U   A r e   N O T   A l o n e

Here Are Some Daily words of encouragement. Repeat Before and After A nap.

MAY I Be Filled with loving·Kindness

MAY I Be well

MAY I Be Peacefully AT eASE

MAY I Be HAPPY

JACK Kornfield
A PATH with HeARt

*You can chAnge I to you To send it out to others

I THINK we need A NATIONAL NAP STAMP! Benefits From it COULD Go toward THE $18 Billion spent Yearly Due to lack of sleep.

OH MY. I Feel A BIG NAP COMING on... You can THINK of Me, napping HAppily and Helplessly in San Francisco. I can iMAGine US LAUGHing together in THE DREAM WORLD!

I send you ABundant and splendid NAps in All sorts of ordinary and unlikely circumstances.

I send you A FAiry lantern To LIGHT your way. let's see WHere our

naps Take us next! NAP on! love,

SARK

 Permission

For:

TO Live long & NAPPY!

# nap resources

## nap equipment

BUCKY: eye pillows,
neck pillows 800·692·8259

Sounds True
Catalog of Healing
Audio Tapes 800·333·9185

SARK nap Blankets + More Gifts
© Impact at 701·255·6410

## NAP MUSIC

CD's:
The Poet     } By Michael Hoppé : Martin Tillman
The Dreamer  } By Michael Hoppé
The Yearning } : Tim Wheater

Saturday Night     By Joshua Kadison
in Storyville      www.joshuakadison.com

Cinema Serenade    By John Williams :
                   Pittsburgh Symphony
                   Orchestra

Song: Nightowl     By Carly Simon

## NAP BOOKS

Dr. Seuss's Sleep Book  By Dr. Seuss

The Napping House       By Audrey Wood
                        illustrated by Don Wood

The Art of Napping      By William Anthony

Spilling Open    By Sabrina Ward Harrison

17 Ways to Eat a Mango  By Joshua Kadison

There is Nothing Wrong With You
                   By Cheri Huber

Hearing Voices    By Brian Andreas
                  800·476·7178

Goodnight Moon  By Margaret Wise Brown

## nap stuff that didn't fit into one of the other pillows

Cards and wise words "For the little
ones inside…" by Robyn Posin
805·646·4518  Box 725 Ojai CA 93024

Channeled Astrology By Rob Breszny
900·903·2500 (worth the Money)

SARK's Inspiration Phone Line
415·546·epic (3742) 24 Hours

The World Nap Organization
an open Society for the Advancement
and Study of Napping.
www.bluemarble.net/~amyloo/wno.html

## We Are All Connected by NAPS

**nap angel** *(left figure)*

**nap angel** *(right figure)*

### To reach us at CAMP SARK

CAMP SARK is a company that designs and creates products for creative living. Our mission is to spread the spirit of SARK - a philosophy that says we are each creatively gifted and need to share those gifts.

CALL: 415. 397. SARK (general information)

Write: CAMP SARK PO BOX 330039 SF CA 94133
(you'll be included in SARK's Magic Mailing list)

E-MAIL: CAMPSARK@BEST.COM

WEB SITE: WWW.CAMPSARK.COM

### To order SARK's inspired Gift collection

look in stores near you!

CARDS, notecards, posters, prints, Blankets and more

**For a Free catalog of SARK Gift items:** call IMPACT at 701·255·6410

if you are a retailer, call
Portal at 800. 227. 1720
or
Rug Barn at 800. 626. 7033

### To order SARK's First 5 Books:

1. A creative companion
2. inspiration sandwich
3. SARK's Journal & play! Book
4. Living juicy
5. The Magic Cottage Address Book

Ask at your favorite Bookstore or call Celestial Arts at

**800. 841. BOOK**

or write PO Box 7327
Berkeley CA 94707

**tiny nap angel**

### To order SUCCULENT WILD WOMAN or THE BODACIOUS BOOK of SUCCULENCE

BOTH BY SARK

CALL Simon & Schuster
**800· 223· 2336**

or write: 200 OLD TAPPAN ROAD
OLD TAPPAN, New Jersey 07675

To order Audiotapes of Creative Companion or Succulent Wild Woman call Audio Literature 800·383·0174

**You are an angel**

### Call for succulent nap inspiration!!

SARK's inspiration phone line 415. 546. 3742 (epic)

Hear a Healing Message, and place for tears and JOY 3-5 minute message by SARK 24 Hours

SARK'S MAGIC Museletter

YOU Are A Gift This

There is a MAGIC COTTAGE INSIDE EACH OF US

DEAR DARLING NAP FACES,

Welcome to your personal invitation to the MAGIC Museletter! I love that while I'm writing, napping and dreaming up new books, we are able to stay connected through the Museletter.

The MAGIC Museletter was born in 1996 and now goes out to many thousands of people around the world. It is the result of a wonder full collaboration between my business partners, the staff of Camp SARK and you. The Museletter is mailed to you quarterly in a handy travel size, making it the perfect napping companion. It is meant to be tasted, nibbled and sipped before or after the perfect nap or whenever you are in need of a burst of inpiration. My favorite ways to read the Museletter are: curled up in the sun, upside down in my pajamas or outside in my garden by moonlight. A subscription to the MAGIC Museletter includes a giant full page, full color letter from me, advanced peeks into my new books, full color artwork and illustrations and chances for you to submit your own artwork and writings!

Until we meet in the Museletter, I send you enlightened lullabies, permission to cry more often, and a MAGIC carpet to nap on.

in NAPPISH SPLENDOR, SARK

Here's what you can look forward to in the Museletter:

🌀 Each issue includes a 17" x 24" Inspirational letter from SARK that focuses on different themes. Some back issues themes have included: Healing, Friendship, Succulence, and Comfort

🌀 SARK's Purple Backpack Adventures–A Traveler's Guide To Serendipity

🌀 Inner Views–Wild Imaginings with highly creative people (which we all are!)

🌀 Subscriber's Contribute–An opportunity for your art and writing to be published in the Museletter!

🌀 SARK's latest calendar & book gathering dates.

🌀 Ripe News from Camp and more!

To order back issues of the Museletter send check or money orders for $4.50 (includes shipping and handling-$6.50 for all foreign orders, in US funds only please!) to Camp SARK, Attn: ML Back issues, PO Box 330039, SF, CA 94133.

ACTUAL SIZE 17x24 INCHES

# Yes!

Please sign me up to receive a two-year, eight-issue subscription of **SARK's Magic Museletter.** Please send this card (see below) and payment to:

### Camp SARK
Attn: Museletter, PO Box 330039,
San Francisco, CA 94133

Rates are as follows: Regular–$23;
"**Star** achie**ving** Artist"–$19.50; Child 12 & Under $19.50; All Foreign Orders–$28 *(payable in U.S. funds only) Checks or money orders accepted. Checks made payable to Camp SARK.*

## Send a Friend a Gift!

There will be so much inspiration and information in **SARK's Magic Museletter,** you'll want to share it with your friends and family. The Museletter is a unique gift to give and to receive. It will provide two years' worth of creativity and fun at a great price! Please choose a rate for your gift subscription and send it along with your payment to the above address. A gift card will be sent to the recipient to announce their new subscription.

Please allow 6-8 weeks for delivery
of your first issue.

---

Gently tear out this page and send it to

# SARK'S Magic Museletter
### Subscriber Information
*(Please print clearly!)*

1

Name
_____

Phone #                              E-mail
_____

Address
_____

City                     State      Zip (+4)
_____

Rates: *(circle one)*
    Regular–$23
    "Starving Artist"–$19.50
    Child 12 & Under $19.50
    All Foreign Orders–$28 *(payable in U.S. funds only)*

2

Name
_____

Phone #                              E-mail
_____

Address
_____

City                     State      Zip (+4)
_____

Rates: *(circle one)*
    Regular–$23
    "Starving Artist"–$19.50
    Child 12 & Under $19.50
    All Foreign Orders–$28 *(payable in U.S. funds only)*

Order 1 is a Gift Subscription* from:
_____

Order 2 is a Gift Subscription* from:
_____

*Checks or money orders accepted. Checks made payable to Camp SARK*
Please allow 6-8 weeks for delivery of your first issue.
*A gift card will be mailed to recipient.